MW01178628

We've never had it so good

Peter M Kitchen

To the U3A

Self-publishing website www.lulu.com

Further copies can be purchased by visiting the above site and entering **We've never had it so good** in the **Find** section.

Copyright, © 2015 by Peter M Kitchen

ISBN: 978-1-326-48577-1

Photographs on the front cover.

Members of the U3A bridge club in the Lindisfarne Room at St Cuthbert's church in Fulwood, Preston.

The camper van, a popular means to get away for weekends and longer breaks.

A leisurely way to see the countryside on our network of canals.

CONTENTS

We've never had it so good

Introduction

Jaques, in William Shakespeare's 'As you Like It', described the seven stages of man. More recently four ages are talked about each lasting about twenty to twenty-five years, defined as preparation, achievement, fulfilment and completion. In this short publication I have condensed life to three phases, not very originally entitled the First, Second and Third Ages, corresponding to childhood and school, college and working life and later years and retirement.

The First Age has often been described as the *Monkey Years*, basically a time for fun with few responsibilities or commitments. This was in complete contrast to the second, the *Donkey Years*, where life could be a constant slog working hard to pay a mortgage and bring up a family.

When you entered the final phase your sons and daughters had normally long fled the nest. If you were fortunate to enjoy good health and to have a loving partner or companion and friends it could be said that you had once again returned to the Monkey Years when, grandparent duties notwithstanding, you could pass the time as you pleased, hopefully to complete a fulfilling and meaningful life We are lucky to have a longer life expectancy rich in possibilities, with a bonus of 20 years or more, not available to previous generations.

As Harold Macmillan said in a 1957 speech "You've never had it so good" and without doubt most of those of us alive at that time had not.

It is my opinion and that of many of my peers that people born in the baby boom, within the eight years or so after the end of World War II and at the time of writing are now pensioners in their sixties, have lived through the most fortunate period in our history with regard to each of these three ages. Pensioners' wealth has increased substantially over the last twenty years and the 'grey pound' accounts for a growing proportion of UK spending. With the many looming problems of population, dwindling resources, climate change and more mundane personal issues such as student loan repayments, soaring property prices and job security, it may also have been the most privileged time for some generations to come.

Whilst these are accounts from my own experiences in the Preston area, I'm sure that they could relate to anywhere else in the country.

This book reflects on the belief that individuals born in that period really have never had it so good.

1. The First Age

We cannot start to imagine the hardship and privation suffered by our parents and grandparents. Having just recovered in the 1920s from the slaughter of the First World War they had to endure the depression of the thirties. Our mothers and fathers, typically born soon after World War I had to face another conflict. Many were forced to move away from the big cities to stay in less dangerous places outside the conurbations with families who often resented the imposition. At the end of the war some had lost fathers, brothers and uncles fighting for their country or people they knew killed or maimed in bombing raids. Rationing continued for several more years.

One thing that they all had in common was that they wanted a better life, in a land fit for heroes, for themselves and their families.

Prior to this time no generation could have any notion about improving their lives. School wasn't regarded as particularly important. You were taught to read and write, do simple arithmetic and learnt stories from the Bible. Apart from the few pupils who passed their 11 plus and went to a grammar school, you continued at the same elementary school and left aged 14 to start earning. There were no secondary schools at that time and no atmosphere of care. My father-in-law struggling to undo his collar at a swimming lesson in the 1920s was thrown into the water. The memory of that incident prevented him from learning to swim or from going to the baths during his adult life. A friend's mother had a pal hit in the eye, causing extensive swelling, during playtime. Instead of calling an ambulance she told the victim to sit at his desk until his mother collected him at the end of lessons. He lost an eye as a result. If any boy from the grammar school was caught talking to a girl from a nearby school it was an instant caning offence.

In those days the father was very much master of the house and many regarded his missus as 'chattel'. Most women ceased to go out to work once they had married and started a family very soon after. The wife and kids had no voice. Pop regularly got out the strap to children in many households and if my father and his brother were playing up they'd be warned "I'll bang your bloody stupid heads together". They would frequently start working in the same factory as their fathers. There was no ambition whatsoever. Career advice would be "Tha's going down t'pit", "Don't marry a farmer" or "What's good enough for me and my father is good enough for thee". Many sons felt the same that what was good enough for their father was indeed good enough for them. Books were few and far between, magazines unknown. In fact many dads took pride in saying "There'll be no books in this house".

Smoking and looking at the newspaper were the main recreations. In the evening, after work, the pub had been the only leisure activity along with going to watch football on a Saturday afternoon.

It was hardly surprising that our parents wanted something else in their lives and by the late fifties there were improvements.

Full employment enabled families to have more money in their pockets.

A great concern that they had was for the infectious diseases of the time - diphtheria, whooping cough and the highly contagious polio. They couldn't march us fast enough to the vaccination clinics that had recently opened to queue for our jabs.

From being a rarity in the early 50s, by the end of the decade most homes had a television set, usually rented from Rediffusion. A monochrome, 14 inch box that took an age to warm up. There were two channels BBC and ITV which you set by moving a dial to 2 or 9. All the roofs now had an aerial shaped like a letter H or X attached to their chimneys. Watching TV became the main occupation in households. 'Andy Pandy' and 'Bill and Ben' were two of the daily 'Watch with mother' programmes for the youngest children and 'Children's Hour' from 5 until 6 o'clock was a treat for the older ones. 'Grandstand' with David Coleman was the Saturday afternoon entertainment. In these early days of television there were lots of westerns being broadcast such as 'Bonanza', 'Rawhide' and the 'Lone Ranger'. Game shows – 'What's my line' and 'Crackerjack' where you received a cabbage for dropping prizes – greens weren't regarded as important then! The ever popular 'This is your life' and 'I love Lucy'.

'Dixon of Dock Green' followed by 'Z Cars' were the precursors of crime and police programmes that were to have such an influence on our screens over the years and 'Coronation Street' from 1960 the first soap opera – still as popular more than fifty-five years on as it was then.

All the northern mill towns had a 'Wakes week' when entire industries and shops in the town closed down for a week. Many families could now afford to go to the seaside for a holiday or for a day out at the weekend. We'd all troop off to the railway station, buckets and spades in hand, to go to a boarding house in Blackpool. Nowadays people jump in the car and can be sixty miles away in an hour using the motorway network. Today the 17 miles to Blackpool is considered a stone's throw and regarded as easy commuting distance to work. At that time the destination was half a day's journey. Places like this were so inaccessible and different from our normal experience to make the beach, amusement arcades with the penny (1d) slot machines and cockle stalls on the promenade seem wonderful. After tea many of the guests would head for the lounge on Mondays and Wednesdays as they could not miss 'Coronation Street' even whilst away. Holiday makers would stroll along the piers to get a glimpse of some of the stars of the day heading to the theatres. One evening we may go to a show with Jimmy Clitheroe or Frankie Vaughan leading the programme.

We started at infant school aged 4. Currently most children start in the September after their 4th birthday – whether they had just turned four or were nearly five. In our day we went at the beginning of the spring, summer or autumn term when we were ready, but before our 5th birthday. Few children had been left at a nursery and it was quite an ordeal to be taken away from their mothers in the first couple of days. Much of that first year in school was spent colouring with crayons or playing with plasticine. We learnt our alphabets using a slate.

There was no formality regarding lessons. Teachers taught more or less as they pleased. If the weather was pleasant in the summer the class would have a stroll along the canal and into the park to play games and collect items for the nature table. There was no extra supervision to handle thirty children and no classroom assistants to help out in the school.

I do recall spelling and mental arithmetic tests on a weekly basis in the later years – long before literacy and numeracy hours. It did make us good 'spellers' and years later employers complained about the poor spelling ability of candidates on the job application forms – even in the days of *Spell Checkers*. Calculating 8 items at a shilling and 7 pence halfpenny (1/7½d) in your head was quite a challenge, particularly when you see people unable to work out how much change to give when £1 is tendered for a 69p sale or use a calculator to add 30p and 40p!

We made extensive use of a 'First Aid in English' book with lots of grounding such as names of groups – a pride of lions, parliament of owls; plurals – mice, geese, oxen and male and female equivalents – nephew and niece and so on. I felt that this gave us excellent general knowledge.

Most schools only had a yard. There were no nearby playing fields in the towns nor grassy areas where you could play football. Rounders was a quite popular recreation for PE lessons along with climbing ropes or folk dancing in the hall.

At play-time several friends would link arms and call "Cowboys and Indians – All join in" or the like to recruit extra children to partake in whatever activity was taking place.

Despite the phenomenal increase in television sets by 1960, every town had several cinemas in its centre and scattered around the municipality. There were no films on the small screen in those days but they would soon take their toll on the picture houses.

On Saturday afternoons masses of youngsters would go to the matinee at the local cinema. Invariably the show would consist of a slapstick comedy with the 'Three Stooges', a 'Pathe News' followed by a cowboy. Children from eight years upwards went on their own. No-one would have dreamt of having their parents take them or collect them afterwards and of course they did not own a car to drop them off. We all had this independence that has disappeared from today's generation. An extra treat on the way was to go into the sweet shop and purchase a penny liquorice stick or a 2d lucky bag containing a few sherbets, fruit salads and a gob stopper.

Nobody thought anything about the walk there as we were all accustomed to getting bread and vegetables at the local shops for our mothers. How often today would you see ten year olds walking on their own to the supermarket, filling a trolley for their parents and then carrying a couple of shopping bags home?

When not at school, all the children in the neighbourhood played out in the vicinity of their homes. Boys and girls of all ages joined in together. Girls constantly bounced balls against the wall with one or two hands and performed handstands. Dolls were clothed and pushed in their prams and sometimes pets also had to tolerate this treatment. Children used to cart wheel across the road. The streets were so quiet at that time in the fifties that it was a rarity if a car went passed in half an hour. The youngsters who lived on a main road simply went round the corner to play outside their friends' houses. Skipping ropes came out along with stilts, hula hoops, spinning tops, yo-yos and a host of other toys. Everyone seemed to carry a few marbles in their pockets and collected chestnuts in the autumn to thread through a string for games of conkers.

Roller skates, scooters and bikes were popular. Best of all was a home-made go-kart – a plank of wood with four pram wheels fitted, upon which you lied down on your stomach and steered with a rope or piece of a washing line. Kids went hurtling down the road. If anyone was up to mischief, throwing stones or making a general nuisance of themselves, a bobby had an uncanny way of appearing and would give the offender a clip round the ear to lessen the likelihood of a repeat.

The streets of terrace houses either had 'backs' at the rear where the back door from the yard led to a narrow ginnel separating houses from the next road or there was a 'lobby', an alley or passage way shared by two adjacent houses to get to their back yards. You could play French cricket in the backs where there was no danger of breaking windows and lads occupied themselves for hours with 'keepy uppy' counting how many times they could kick a football off their feet without it touching the floor.

All the families struggled for money. Clothes were passed down from older siblings and neighbours would help one another and there were always patches on sleeves and holes in jumpers and plimsolls. Children shared the same bedroom.

There couldn't be a greater contrast between this community fun that we enjoyed and the lack of activities outside their homes of youngsters today. The quiet roads of yesteryear and often the pavements are now regularly infested with cars. Even in leafy avenues it is a rarity to see children playing outside their home. One wonders how they pass the time other than by sending silly texts to one another, looking at Facebook on their mobiles that are seldom put away or watching their own televisions and playing games on their X Boxes in their 'private space'.

Not all our time was spent outdoors. If it was wet we played in one another's houses. Meccano sets were very popular and loads of boys had partially completed models in their rooms. Some extra parts were often bought with any spare pocket money. We all did jigsaws and some of us had a 'compendium of games' consisting of a dozen or more board games such as draughts, chess or solitaire and instructions for a variety of games with playing cards. Comics were exchanged to discover the latest antics of Desperate Dan and Biffo the bear.

From a very young age we were taken to the local park by our mothers. They would take us to the aviaries or push us on the swings and roundabouts. In addition some had a paddling pool and sand pit where we had the time of our lives.

When we were old enough to take ourselves there we would roly-poly down the grassy slopes, play leapfrog, hide and seek and learnt to swing ourselves sitting or standing up. We would find trees to climb and make dens in the bushes from branches and rose bay willow herb stems. Often someone would bring a kite to fly.

One of the bunch would always carry a net and a jam jar to try to bring back a few tadpoles. Others would bring a match box in which to take home a caterpillar and a couple of leaves on which it was feeding. We'd keep them in a goldfish bowl with a piece of wood on top in a shed or lean-to and inspect them daily to see the tadpoles beginning to sprout legs and the caterpillar becoming a chrysalis and if we were lucky turn into a moth or butterfly.

These experiences, such a vital part of our growing up, seem to be totally absent from the lives of today's youngsters.

A recent addition for many households was the transistor radio. Whilst insignificant compared to the ghetto blasters a few years later it was a fantastic gadget that could be carried around from room to room. Mum could listen to her favourite programmes during the day whilst ironing and dad could tune in to the football results on Saturdays. The whole family would listen to 'Two Way Family Favourites', 'The Billy Cotton Band Show' on a Sunday and the highlight of the week, 'Pick of the Pops'.

We were allowed to take the radio to our bedrooms to listen to Radio Luxemburg. Late at night we'd listen to it under the bed sheets. Reception in the summer was dreadful but it was terrific - a 'Personal source of music' – akin to an IPod forty years later.

Pop music had started to really take off at this time. Elvis Presley and Cliff Richard and the Shadows had begun to make a name but the phenomenon of the 'groups' was yet to come. By the early sixties the Beatles, Cilla Black and Gerry and the

13

Pacemakers had put Liverpool firmly on the map and the scene had changed out of all recognition within a few years with new groups from all over the country.

This coincided with a new breed 'Teenagers'. It was never clear when the word was introduced - there were always adolescents in their teens - but it was a time when people of that age had more of their own money to spend and wanted to be independent of their parent's ideals. They had their own language. Parents were regarded as 'square'. We were having 'a gas'. That's 'groovy'. Do you not dig what we're saying? Words that would now make you cringe or 'ROFL' compared to today's 'gr8' 'text and facebook speak'. They had individualised fashion emulating the pop stars, taken from Carnaby Street, with miniskirts as short and lads' hair as long as possible.

The era became known as the 'Swinging Sixties'. For many of us it was the best time of our lives with dramatic changes in all areas with music of the period still being regularly played 50 years later.

Many families moved away from their urban terraced house with an outside toilet and back yard to a semi-detached dwelling in the suburbs with a garden. This was a wonderful improvement from only a few years before. At last soft paper replace the rough 'Izal'!

In the home lots of 'Mod Cons' had been bought though it was still a long way from a 'Consumer Society'. Telephones, washing machines and refrigerators had become common place.

Gas fires and central heating were replacing the arduous and time consuming efforts of making a fire on a winter's morning.

Lots of younger people with families were taking the opportunity of learning to drive and purchasing a car. As well as replacing those journeys previously made by bus or train it opened up avenues never previously available such as picnics and day trips into the countryside or coast and holidays to distant corners of Britain.

At primary school we still took an 11+ examination in what is now known as year six. Usually three or four were successful and went to a grammar school. There were separate establishments for boys and girls and for catholic and C of E faiths. Although some pupils remained at the school, most others went to one of the new secondary moderns that had recently opened. This ensured that they weren't written off for failing the 11+ and many of them took O-levels or CSEs. The brightest students had the opportunity of transferring to the sixth form at the grammar schools. The whole system was replaced soon after with comprehensive education providing schools for all levels of ability.

School uniform costs were astronomic. There was no such things as discount stores and they had to be purchased at a limited number of outlets and the total could amount to several weeks' wages.

In those days we weren't allowed to use a biro except for rough work. Homework had to be handed in written with a fountain pen. Everyone carried a bottle of 'Quink' ink with which to fill their pens. A great improvement was the cartridge pen that led to a lot less blotches and the need for blotting paper. Although virtually unknown today, it did help make people have better handwriting.

Almost all pupils had pastimes and hobbies. The most common were sport (watching and playing), fishing, nature, collecting items and spotting. These interests could lead to great skills, knowledge and expertise in later years.

Many in the class watched their local football team and those with the greatest ability played football and cricket, netball and hockey or took part in athletics for the school teams and in local clubs. Of course they still do today but the big difference is that all the games are organised for them. It is rare to see a dozen lads arranging their own informal game of football on the park with jumpers for the goal posts or playing cricket with a tree substituting for the stumps and wicket keeper.

Fishing at the time was very popular. Often the whole family would take to the canal side and have a picnic and a stroll whilst the male side of the family stared at their floats for hours on end. In the summer months lads would carry their rods for an hour's fishing by a nearby bridge. It is now a rarity to see more than the occasional fisherman there, yet fifty years ago you had sometimes to walk quite a distance along the towpath to find a spare place.

At least the canals themselves see far greater use nowadays. They are popular for walkers and cyclists where the paths provide miles of a traffic free area and keen sailors take to their boats on the waters to see the countryside at a leisurely pace.

A casual interest in nature, picking flowers or observing voles, dragonflies and swallows by the stream, river or canal side could lead to a lifetime's involvement in conservation or expertise in ornithology.

Nearly everybody in the class seemed to have an interest in collecting things. Stamps were the most popular item, usually starting with a 6d packet of a mixture of foreign ones bought from Woolworth's (where you got most things) and an album that might have had its origins in a Christmas stocking. This could lead to a specialisation assembling those from particular countries.

Other items were coins, football programmes from an assortment of clubs, fag packets and I remember one classmate having a collection of different newspapers, mostly local papers from towns around Britain.

Although cigarette cards had long disappeared, you could buy bubble gum which had a flag-card with each purchase. These had a picture of the flag from one of eighty countries. If you bought more than a couple, the shopkeeper would give you a few extra cards. On the back various information was supplied such as its capital, population, location and monetary unit.

Brooke Bond tea provided a card with every packet. Each was in a series of 50, lasting for about six months before a new category was issued. Most were of wildlife such as British mammals or tropical birds. In recent years other topics were included – history of the motor car or inventions for example. You could obtain booklets in which to stick them or just keep them together with an elastic band.

All the various collectibles could be exchanged or sold in the classroom before assembly. Quite apart from the enjoyment derived from the collections there were tremendous educational benefits.

Spotting and writing down numbers was immensely popular. Long before *Stagecoach*, virtually every town with a populace of 50,000 or so had its own fleet of corporation buses. It was easy to collect their numbers and complete the set. More interesting and challenging was to attempt to see all the buses in a municipal fleet such as *Ribble*, numbering over 1000, that transported passengers in the area outside the towns and had garages scattered across the county. Ian Allan Books were widely available that listed every class, number and registration of each vehicle with details of when and by whom they were built. You would underline them once you had spotted them.

Observing car registrations, looking for those with foreign number plates and the country of origin or attempting to see a number plate with a 1, then a 2 and so on in sequence was also commonplace. Whilst some had given up by the time they had reached double figures, others continued for several years finally getting to 999 – or even beyond. Quite apart from the lack of interest in such activities these days, it is obviously not practicable. People tend to look instead for celebrity or amusing plates where the owners have paid substantial amounts for registrations such as FE ll OWS or HA lO EEN.

These activities paled into insignificance compared to the most prevalent pastime of the era – trainspotting. Each form in the school would have several spotters who spent a high proportion of any spare hour by the lineside.

It is hard to believe today that every bridge and recreation area was a meeting point for the hordes of railway fanatics who lived in the vicinity. Almost every bit of their free time was spent there. A spell before tea, in the evening after completing homework until it was dark and on Saturdays. Conversations took place between friends about what unusual locomotives had been noted. Dozens of others stood at the end of station platforms discussing their latest 'cops' or engines that they had never seen before. These locations are deserted today and the only enthusiasts that you see on a platform tend to be elderly men of our age group.

However there is still an interest in railways. If there is a steam hauled special train, or even a former BR diesel on an outing, the bridges are once more packed with age ranges varying from parents with their young children, to middle aged 'professional photographers' and folks in their eighties reminiscing about the good old days. Many of the staff at the preserved railway centres were born long after the era of steam engines and increasingly diesel and electric locos had ended.

Parents in the 1950s and 60s were very happy for their sons to have a hobby that fully occupied them. Many of the grammar schools had a railway society and organised coach trips known as 'shed bashes' to other parts of the country where engine sheds and works were visited legally with a permit. This was quite different from the way that we used to sneak round some of the depots. Steam would be billowing out, there was smoke everywhere and piles of hot ash deposited by the tracks. We just casually strode past it all – there was no health and safety in those days!

Although difficult to believe today, as 12 and 13 year olds we travelled across the country, making our way through cities such as Leeds and Manchester to sheds or would plonk ourselves on trolleys at the end of busy stations in York or Doncaster.

Even more incredible, whilst climbing onto engines on the scrap line in the local shed – 'cabbing them' as it was known, we were often invited onto the footplate by a driver and his fireman and journeyed to the sidings to pick up some waggons. This would be inconceivable nowadays. They would be instantly dismissed and probably arrested as suspected child molesters. At the time it was treated as perfectly normal behaviour and the crew would no doubt have their own sons taking part in similar activities.

Once they reached the age of 15 or 16 groups of between two and four boys or girls partook in their first independent holidays away from their parents, youth hostelling. Some groups cycled but the majority planned a walking holiday, trekking from one hostel to another using tracks and footpaths in the countryside. You were expected to reach the first hostel using public transport and then continue under your own steam. In the 1960s no-one was allowed to bring a car to a hostel!

Prices were very cheap - costing about 5 or 6 shillings a night. If you made a reservation in advance you would send a postal order – now barely heard of. You could purchase a breakfast and a dinner for about 3 or 4 shillings. Alternatively you could cook your own meals using the kitchen facilities. During the evening we used to mix with others of a similar age in the lounge. Cards and board games were generally available with magazines and copies of *Readers Digest*. I cannot recall of any having a television.

You slept in a dormitory consisting typically of about six bunk beds. Everybody had to carry around a sheet sleeping bag that you placed on the bed under blankets that were provided to avoid contaminating the bedding. 'Lights out' took place promptly at 10.30pm.

Before checking out in the morning and getting your membership card returned you had to ask "What's my job?" These were usually sweeping the dorm or scrubbing frying pans. Occasionally it was hard labour such as filling coal buckets! This was to ensure that the business could be run on a shoestring. When you had performed your chore your card was stamped with the youth hostel's name and badge and you could be on you way.

Times change. Only a decade or so later the majority of YHA members were in their twenties and it became the norm for the young adults to drive there or tour around. Now there are family and private rooms. You no longer help to maintain the place and prices have risen steeply – sometimes being comparable to a cheap bed and breakfast residence. For many years now, no-one under the age of 18 can actually go hostelling unless accompanied by an adult.

This century they have been modernised further with the abolition of communal wash rooms and the sleeping bag and beds are already made up for you on arrival.

To provide money for our expeditions we had a Post Office savings account. You would regularly invest any spare income that had been obtained from paper rounds or presents at the local post office. At the time these were the only places not only where you could buy stamps but also general stationery such as envelopes.

There would always be a post office wherever you happened to be on your travels to take out some cash. You could make only one withdrawal per day of up to £3 and £5 on a single occasion during the week. ATMs or Cash Machines were unknown.

School life was about to finish, the end of the *monkey years* and time to face the outside world.

2. The Second Age

The school leaving age had not been raised to 16 in the 1960s and most pupils with no academic inclination left, aged 15 having not taken any examinations whatsoever. For the last two or three years more practical lessons had been on offer – carpentry, metalwork, cookery and needlework as being of greater benefit. Unlike today there were lots of unskilled jobs available. Countless girls were employed in shops or as factory workers and lads took up apprenticeships in whatever major employers happened to be in the town or became involved in the transport industry. Many loaded lorries, assisted van drivers with deliveries or underwent training to become mechanics. The most remarkable thing was how so many people could pack up a job one week to have no difficulty starting fresh employment the next.

Those who did carry on for another year sat O-levels or CSEs and the equivalent of 5 passes could lead to work in almost any field and had the same buying power as a degree today – starting to earn five years earlier and with no loan to repay.

Positions as shorthand typists, secretaries and receptionists were very popular for the young women. There were careers for both sexes in major stores, banks, building societies, estate agents and in the public sector areas of the health service, local government and the civil service. Private businesses were crying out for bright young school leavers. Most training was 'on the job' and those wishing to progress could continue at night school classes.

Remaining at school and studying for A-levels was generally restricted to the top couple of streams at the grammar schools. Subject choices were quite limited to three science subjects, languages, classics or the arts. Taking your education further and going on to university was by no means an automatic option. Those of us who did were in a small minority and regarded themselves as very fortunate. Only those who wished to have a vocation in areas such as medicine and law or to become an engineer took subjects for a specific reason. The rest simply applied for the subject that they liked and were good at without the faintest thought concerning what to do at the end of the course.

Holiday jobs were plentiful and you would meet up with many former school chums whilst working in the sorting office for a couple of weeks when the Christmas mail was at its busiest.

When we applied to university via the UCCA system, that handled the applications, many of the establishments made you an offer without meeting you at all. At others you had to attend for an interview and have a look around if you were interested. Following the visit, if the university wanted you they would frequently make you an easy offer of just 2 or 3 grade E's to entice you or 3 A's as a deterrent.

At the start of your college life a few days were taken up with what is known as 'Fresher's Week'. In addition to taking up your accommodation and registering, you opened up a current account for the first time in which you would deposit your grant cheque.

There was also a big assembly hall, like an exhibition centre today, with tables and desks for the dozens of interests and leisure activities being handled by the club secretaries and aficionados. There was the opportunity to carry on with your favourite sports or try new ones such as basketball or judo. Bridge and chess clubs were ever present, rambling societies and a choir and orchestra for the musically minded. At that time there was always a railway society – but supporters' interests had matured from spotting to transport history and amassing an impressive collection of photographs where changes to the network were occurring.

Whilst I have no doubt that much of this still takes place for the current intake I find it sad when some students tell us that the main activities during that week seem to be spending large sums of money travelling by coach to hostelries and getting legless!

The university population at many of the big cities at that time was about six thousand. We thought it was huge but minute compared to those of today where numbers may exceed 30,000. If you applied early enough it was fairly easy to get accommodation in one of the purpose built halls of residence or lodgings near to the lecture theatres if you preferred. Many stayed in the halls for the full three years of their course whilst others chose to share a rented flat in their final year.

Looking back, it is hard to credit what a luxurious life it was in the halls. Breakfast and an evening meal provided for us every day with full board at the weekends. Our bedding changed, daily newspapers on hand, games rooms with table tennis, snooker and pool and a bar. The social committee organised the showing of a blockbuster film each week.

We took it all for granted, almost treating it as a right and never pausing to reflect about how lucky we were.

For many years now any spare ground has been converted to student apartments where it is all self-catering and where several rooms share communal cooking facilities.

In our day every student received an award from the local education authority. The amount that you received was assessed depending upon you parents' income with a maximum of about £400. There was also a minimum amount of £50 – even for a millionaire. Nobody paid fees. In fact it never occurred to most students that there was such a thing as *fees* – it just 'happened' in the same manner as schools received money for lessons.

Not only was there a grant but students who had to spend more than £12 a year travelling to and from the institution from home each term or from their digs every day received a 'travelling allowance'. If you had to stay for an extra week as part of the curriculum or had to buy specialised materials you could make a claim for these.

Today's students cannot believe the halcyon days that we revelled in. Large numbers supplement their income by taking a part-time job in the evening – generally bar work. With fees of up to £9000 a term and maintenance costs the loan to be repaid can be in excess of £40,000.

After graduation our next concern was obtaining employment. Each week the colleges would issue a list of vacancies with the requirements that applicants must have. We looked for others in the local paper.

At that time many large employers and especially the public sector were expanding their workforce and looking for graduates in areas such as administration, accountancy and other facets of finance, personnel, all aspects of computing, trainee management and engineering. By the end of the summer most had started work in an area where their subject at least bore a connection. Whilst some were happy to work anywhere in the country where there was a vacancy most stayed near their home town, in the city in which they had received their degree or in London and the south east.

Your occupation gave you a wealth of opportunities. The high flyers intent on reaching the top as a head teacher, company director, bank manager or being in charge of their own business were willing to uproot themselves several times, hundreds of miles across the country or abroad to achieve their goal.

The majority, perhaps after a couple of job changes, were content to make a slow but steady progress up the ladder. Some remained in academia at their college in a research field. One colleague, a brilliant artist, was willing to simply perform tasks as directed by his manager provided that he had an income sufficient to allow him to pursue his passion of sitting by his easel painting.

Others with no proclivity for materialism or a desire to earn a lot of money but with a love of the outdoors became rangers or involved in countryside management.

We were extremely lucky to have these choices. Jobs were not too hard to come by and we did not owe anything. With the enormous numbers graduating today, hundreds may be applying for the same post. Even with top degrees, most get no further than the on-line application. Those that were interviewed regularly had experience or could offer something special. There were always those that had the knack for saying the right thing, would excel in any aptitude tests and surpass the efforts of other candidates.

Lots are forced to take employment wherever they can, joining people with no degree, in stores, supermarkets or bars, earning a minimum wage or had a soul destroying job at a call centre trying to sell double glazing to a hostile public. Often extending late into the evening necessitating the use of a car to get there. This may increase their debt, already high resulting from their student days that they would have to repay as soon as their salary was sufficiently high. It could take months or even years to obtain the kind of work that they were seeking. The location may then be in one of the big cities forcing a long drive or train journey, with the inconvenience and expense, to get there.

In our day, although the great majority aspired to become a car-owner, there was no need to have to possess one immediately. If the factory or office was 'out of the way' there were always workers' buses to get you there and back.

When we were in our twenties many of us shared a rented house or apartment and were planning to get married. We would look at properties within two or three miles from work. After finding one suitable an appointment would be made at a building society to arrange a mortgage. Unlike today at least one of you had to have been placing their savings there. You had to put down a 10% deposit to receive a loan of 2½ times the man's salary. Your future wife's income would not be taken into account.

A typical salary might be £3000. If you had a £1000 deposit you would receive a loan of £7500. This would be a repayment mortgage with the same building society over 25 years, typically requiring a monthly repayment of £80 that would go up or down depending upon the interest rate. If rates were reduced you would usually try to maintain the same payment so that the loan would be repaid early and you would never be over stretched.

This would be sufficient to purchase a house to the value of £8500 and hopefully between you there would be something left over for furniture. That sum of money would enable you to typically buy a three bedroom semi-detached house in the suburbs with a garden, suitable for bringing up a family. You expected to live there for many years, being able to make an easy journey to work. In the current climate, businesses relocate, are taken over or staff have to move on for a promotion or to develop a career. A thirty mile journey with all the hassle that it entails is commonplace and many firms require employees to travel to appointments with clients the length and breadth of the country.

The same house today in Northern Britain might cost £140,000 and vastly more in the southern counties. To fund a comparable deposit and repayments, with other commitments and outgoings, would be far harder and be totally dependent upon two incomes. You would have to seek out the best mortgage, often short term, at a fixed or variable rate. Regularly it would have to be renegotiated after a couple of years and may entail a surcharge or fee if you changed the provider for a better deal.

To make things harder still, so many jobs are 'zero hours', part-time or temporary contracts that banks, building societies and finance houses are reluctant to make a loan at all. Those positions that were regarded as 'secure' no longer enjoy that luxury with the risk of some of the work being 'off-shored'.

When folk had a family, in almost all circumstances the wife ceased to go out to work and the man became the sole breadwinner. There was no such thing as 'paternity leave'. You saved up leave from your holiday entitlement for when your child was born. Belts had to be tightened of course, but people expected to be hard up for a number of years and budgeted carefully. All the neighbours were in the same boat and life did become a slog – 'the donkey years'. Crèches and child minders were virtually unknown. Only families where the wife was in a very senior post could employ a 'nanny' to manage the house, cook and do the shopping in addition to looking after the children.

When the kids were young you both tended to have an evening out each week on separate days. It might be in a pub dart's team or at a badminton club. A Saturday night out was dependent upon getting a babysitter and we enjoyed passing Sundays together spending precious time as a family visiting relatives, going to a playground at a park or playing games at home. We kept a careful check on our expenditure ensuring that we were living within our means.

Today's situation bears little resemblance to those times. Couples have become used to an existence that two good incomes and a demanding job can bring. They are expected to borrow and 'have it now'. In particular those who had postponed having a family until later in life were often already accustomed to a wealthy life style of detached houses, two new cars, expensive meals out and exotic holidays.

Women are expected to resume working after a spell of maternity leave with their partner also receiving some paternity entitlement. The pressures can be enormous. Getting the children ready early in the morning, taking them to a child-minder, nursery or to a breakfast-club in school and then battling with traffic to get to work. After a hard day there is a repeat performance with additional tasks such as shopping, the gym and transporting the family to a variety of activities thrown in. There are also extra problems if the kids or the carer were poorly and traffic hold-ups to create yet more strain with grandparents regularly called in to ease the burden.

Unsurprisingly this can cause fatigue, stress and difficulties for any relationship. Large numbers break down and face the complications of becoming a single parent. Many say that they'd love to stay at home with the kids but cannot afford to as much of their income is already committed before being received. With extra funding being made to help with child-care, those women that do finish working and want to be a traditional home-maker and be with their children sometimes regard themselves as 'Second class citizens'.

In our day, when the children had reached junior school most women did return to part-time work either as casual employment or to gradually return to that which they had left several years prior. We were typically in our mid to late thirties and considerably better off than we had been for many years. We had more time for ourselves. Many were now helping to run the sports clubs and societies that they had been attending with impressive handicaps at golf, reasonable players in the local football league or experts in their hobbies and able to make a major contribution. In today's climate few from the younger end are coming through to societies so that the committees tend to consist of predominantly older folk – sometimes the same people that had managed things thirty years earlier!

The possessions that had begun to make a difference to people's standard of living in the sixties and make life comfortable had accelerated immensely by the eighties. We were blessed to have lived through the era when we could take advantage of these developments. Almost all homes now had a colour television and four channels had become available. A great asset was the innovation of the video recorder enabling individuals to pre-set something to be watched later or tape one programme whilst viewing another. Unimaginable not many years before. At the same time the transistor radios, reel-to-reel tape recorder and record players were soon superseded by stereo systems with more reliable cassettes and later compact discs. Go forwards another twenty years and the situation became unrecognizable once more with flat screens, cable, satellite dishes and dozens of channels to choose from.

Whilst almost all families had a refrigerator, freezers had not appeared on the landscape until this time. Many packets of frozen vegetables and meat could now be kept and this was of great advantage to those who grew fruit and vegetables in their garden or allotment.

From the days when housewives had to buy groceries for their meals virtually every day of the week, supermarkets were springing up in any available space around towns enabling you to buy a week's supply at reduced prices and store them in the newly acquired deep freeze. Another purchase that took off was the microwave. This time saving device enabled you to cook ready prepared or frozen meals in minutes and was a fantastic benefit for those arriving home from work tired and not feeling inclined to slave over a cooker.

This reminds me of a tale that a teacher friend passed on. The class were learning about the items sold by the different kinds of shops such as a greengrocer or chemist. "Where would you buy meat?" she asked, anticipating an answer of "at a butcher's". "Sainsbury's was the reply". "OK, where would you get a stamp?" "Sainsbury's". "Where would you buy a newspaper?" You've guessed it and it transpired that there wasn't any item from cosmetics to clothing or electrical goods that could not be bought at whichever happened to be mum's favourite supermarket. This culminated on another occasion when the class were learning about the times of year when you gave things such as mother's day presents or put up a tree at

Christmas. "Who can tell me when we buy hot cross buns?" "When they're half price at Sainsbury's!"

A great contribution that the supermarkets made, even in the early days, was to be open into the evening until 8pm allowing the whole family to make the expedition after tea. In the past all local stores and shops in the town centres closed at 6 o'clock at the latest. The extension to Sunday trading and 24 hour opening in some superstores was inconceivable in the past. Whilst grapes used to be reserved for visiting patients in hospital, pineapples and kiwi fruits and exotic vegetables are freely available at all times of the year.

Years ago pubs were no more than drinking houses. Smoke filled, they were inhospitable to families. Rigid hours when they were allowed to serve, until throwing out time at 10.30 in the evening. The last bus to get you home ran at 11pm. Few served food. The nearest to it would be a packet of crisps or a meat and potato pie at lunch time.

We have seen vast improvements in our lifetimes where most serve excellent meals, all day at weekends, and welcome families with an optional public bar and games room maintaining the pub's tradition. The smoking ban has greatly contributed to improving people's health.

From the days when virtually the only cafés were Wimpy bars and Fish and Chip shops the only 'Takeaways' and finding an 'eatery' on a Sunday was near impossible, we have seen wonderful advances. Town centres and every shopping area have a wide selection of places at which to dine or buy a snack to take out. All palettes are provided for with garlic bread,

34

pizzas and pasta dishes, Chinese and Indian cuisines supplementing traditional food. Vegetarians, vegans and customers requesting a gluten free diet are well catered for and items clearly marked if they contain nuts for those with allergies.

Apart from skilled carpenters who could manufacture their own furniture from planks of wood most of us had to have the completed article delivered. DIY stores spread in a similar fashion to the supermarkets, where you could buy flat-packed items cheaper and load them directly into your car with everything that you needed to assemble it incorporated in the one package.

In the 1960s few people had taken a holiday abroad. By the eighties package holidays had become affordable and vacations to the Spanish *costas* or the Greek islands had become commonplace.

Again, at this time in the 1980s, to most of the population the computer was a large, mysterious contraption stuck away in a purpose built room with magnetic tapes whizzing around and costing hundreds of thousands of pounds. Only specialists had the necessary expertise to make them operate. No-one could have even dreamt that twenty years later they would become as essential part of the fittings in the home as an armchair.

We are fortunate once more to have been part of this digital revolution that has transformed lives.

The earliest computers for the home were merely machines with a cassette that enabled you to play a few games. In a short time this has expanded to the laptops of today that can download films and have thousands of times the storage of the gigantic machines that used to run all the administration for large businesses thirty years ago. From being unknown in the early 1990s the internet dominates everything from making purchases, paying bills and seeking information of any description.

The cameras of the past with films that would enable you to take twenty snaps that you had to take to a chemist or photographic shop to be developed have been swept aside by digital cameras with a memory card that would hold over a thousand photos that you can instantly view and delete if not up to scratch.

The previous problems of needing to make a phone call when in a remote area have been completely removed by the advent of the mobile with its fantastic developments in only a few years when it has become the all-embracing device of today for music, photos, emails, Facebook and google.

However in my opinion the greatest improvement of all in our adult lives has been that of equal opportunities and in particular the way in which persons with any 'impediment' or being 'different' in any manner are now treated.

In the early seventies when I began work at an insurance company male graduates commenced with a starting salary of about £1400. Women starting with identical qualifications commenced on £400 per annum less. They could not apply for any position that required shift working. A colleague informed me about one office some years earlier that would not accept females as there were no ladies' toilets! The Equal Pay Act came into force in 1975.

In the 1960s colour and race prejudice was rife with many shops unwilling to serve people that they regarded as 'black' and property owners had signs refusing to let to 'coloured's'. Fortunately all this changed and despite the influx from eastern European nations few people would even notice someone's ethnicity.

At this time anybody with lesbian or homosexual leanings would be very afraid of allowing their feelings to become known because of the abuse that they would attract and sometimes not even be accepted by their families. The 'Gay Rights' movements have enabled them to become completely open and recognized by society as being no different from one individual having blond hair and the next being a brunette with same sex couples able to marry.

Facilities for those with a physical disability have improved by leaps and bounds over this period.

Before this time people confined to a wheel-chair were expected to remain restricted with very limited access to amenities that the rest of the public could enjoy.

The entrances to buildings regularly involved climbing steps or had a narrow revolving door with no alternative means of entry. 'Public Conveniences' in the town centres frequently involved descending a flight of stairs. Due in no small measure to the campaigner, MP Jack Ashley, disabled members of the public have vastly improved services.

Most places now have a slope as an alternative to steps and accessible toilets. Supermarkets provide specially designed wheelchairs at the door that have a built-in shopping basket. 'Motorbility Shops' supply supports for all kinds of disability and battery operated wheel chairs at reasonable prices to provide some freedom. Stannah Stairlifts can be easily fitted onto almost all staircases enabling those with reduced mobility to remain in their own home and maintain their independence. The *Blue Badge* has become indispensable

Previously totally inaccessible 'public' toilets in Fishergate, Preston

Buses have designated areas for push chairs, walking aids and seating reserved for the elderly or those with limited mobility.

Airports especially have staff on hand to assist and there is always a fast-track for young families or people with sticks or other difficulties to go through to the check-ins.

Particularly impressive is the manner in which it has become the norm to assist or give up a seat whenever needed. There is as almost as much interest in the Paralympics as the Olympic Games themselves with many of the public impressed by the records being not far short of those of the able-bodied competitors.

The development of sub-titles on television enormously improved the lives of the deaf and hard of hearing. Conferences regularly employ an expert in sign language so that everyone can participate.

The most recent improvements in IT, the reductions in price and the variety of portable devices that are now available have enabled files and the internet to be accessed from almost anywhere. Hotels, cafeterias and trains have WIFI so that jobs can be done on the journey to meetings or at an overnight stay. Staff often work from home, saving time. This is a huge bonus to people with young families and the self-employed who can labour at the times that suit them.

3. The Third Age.

As we moved into this century many of the people in this book, particularly those who did not enter further education, had been working for well over 30 years. There was a considerable split between the ones who had been with the same employer, able to work overtime when needed and those, especially in heavy industry, who had been made redundant in the period as mills closed or drastically reduced their workforce. The new light industries and distribution centres that tended to supersede the former mining and ship-building sites were often relatively low paid. They frequently necessitated the use of computers and were quite alien to that group at first. However a large proportion were able to adapt their skills.

During discussions with ex-colleagues we have sometimes thought "What work could we have possibly have done if we had been in this predicament?"

Over the next decade the public sector and other large employers were looking to make a severe reduction in staffing to save costs. Rather than make wholesale lay-offs the first option was generally to ask if any staff wished to leave voluntarily. A handful at the younger end, who had become disillusioned, chose to depart with their severance pay-out for new ventures. The second was to request that those approaching retirement age finish prematurely. A high proportion of employees in these firms received a pension at sixty. Personnel approaching this age who did take early retirement were entitled to receive the pension that had been accrued to that time when they finished. Some also received a handsome redundancy pay-out. This enabled their employers to make a reshuffle of posts, reduce layers of management, close branch offices and merge departments.

Whilst for many this was the opportunity for which they had been longing, for a proportion it could be a disaster. They had lived to work rather than the opposite and received a great buzz from the pressures and problem solving, with not much thought as to what to do next and often resorted to passing the mornings goggling at the squabbles on Jeremy Kyle!

Another section, where their pension was insufficient to meet their everyday expenses or who missed the banter and company of colleagues, regularly took the opportunity of part-time employment at large stores and supermarkets whose policies helped provide jobs for unemployed and older people.

For the majority that day couldn't arrive soon enough. Typically aged about sixty and having been careful with money for much of their lives, perhaps making sound investments or taking out bonds when interest rates were higher and now reaping the rewards, it provided the chance to do those things that they had been dreaming about. Once again people in our age group just happened to be around at the right time. Women received their state pension at 60 whilst for men it was 65. Both genders who are now 60 (in 2015) will receive no pension until they reach 66 rising to 68 for people in their early fifties.

For those who remained employed, in the state sector in particular, there had been a fundamental 'job evaluation' that would provide a simplified structure comparing posts throughout the business and form a new grading structure. The effect was that a large percentage of positions would be paid a lower salary than they had received previously. On top of that there were to be continual cuts in government spending. It was felt that there was no longer any job that was safe. Most staff that had been the 'right age' had already finished – there was no silver left to be sold.

For several years annual pay awards had been capped at zero or at most one per cent. The private sector too had received no increases. Although the rise in the cost of living had been very low for the past few years, pensioners had received a yearly increase of the rate of inflation as a minimum.

Extra bonuses were the reduced rates offered to our age group. 10% Wednesday discounts at B&Q, lower prices at leisure centres, museums, barbers' shops and for some concerts and cinema tickets with special 'Pensioners Afternoons' when £5 lets you see a film with a cup of tea and biscuit included. There are the exemptions from prescription and eye-test charges. By far the greatest boon has been the free bus pass and also for local rail services in some of the largest metropolises. Many use the bus pass to get out and about, hopping from one place of interest to the next and to relieve their own sons and daughters by taking grandchildren into town. In fact one feels that the decline in the town centres would have been even more pronounced were it not for these older folk heading to Marks and Spencer's cafeteria.

Previously, when their only source of income was their state pension the elderly were unquestionably hard-up and not infrequently cut down on food so that they had enough money to pay their heating bills. Although no longer earning, in recent times the combination of their monthly retirement income, lump sum that they may have received on finishing work and any money that they had saved or inherited from deceased relatives suddenly made today's aged very well-off, many making generous payments to help their own children.

In the past pensioners tended to be regarded by the general public as 'old'. They thought of themselves in the same light and dressed accordingly in the manner of Nora Batty with wrinkly stockings and clothes to intentionally look unattractive. Now they no longer consider themselves as ancient and can wear glamorous dresses like their daughters and granddaughters and the men sport sandals and shorts for their everyday attire into their seventies and beyond. Many have kept extremely fit and remain athletic - even running marathons! Blood donors too have been treated as young because the age at which they can donate has recently risen to at least 70.

Although influenced by numerous factors and still very much a lottery, the life expectancy of someone aged 60 is now about 82 for a male and 84 for a female. They may be able to pursue an active life-style over the period. This provides some wonderful opportunities that many relish. Keeping healthy by regular swimming, rambles in the countryside, dancing, gardening and competitive sports, albeit at a slower pace than in the past, are common and many take part in voluntary work in the churches helping to raise funds for worthwhile causes at home and overseas, charity shops or environmental projects. Keeping a dog for company and exercise is a great way to make certain that you get out of the house on a daily basis.

By far the most popular is the chance to travel, no longer restricted to school holidays, weekends or office commitments. For the keen drivers a caravan or camper van provides an excellent way of taking short breaks or touring the British Isles or Europe for weeks at a time. City breaks, prolonged stays soaking up the winter sunshine in Tenerife or cruises allowing the prospect of seeing the world and it is not unknown to take four or five vacations a year – combinations of coach trips and holidays abroad. The oft quoted cliché "I don't know how I had time to go to work" was never truer. Time flies past ever more quickly and everyone has a calendar or diary to enable them to keep track of their engagements.

Whilst it is easy to think of this as extravagant, many contemplate on how long they have left and intend to live life to the full whilst they can and to ensure that they have no regrets about deferring those things that they could have done – if only they had made the effort. We all know of people who were completely well one minute and had suddenly suffered a heart attack or discovered that they had cancer.

About 25% of the population is 60 or over, greater than the number under 18, and anticipated to reach 20 million by 2030. Those over 85 are projected to nearly double by this date. The NHS provides a fantastic service for us. Well-man and well-woman clinics provide precautionary examinations hopefully to prevent future ailments and the need to be admitted into hospital.

They give advice and smear tests, checks for bowel cancer, diabetes, cholesterol and other blood tests are routinely performed along with the annual flu injection.

A great proportion already go to social clubs and institutions such as the W.I. The U3A, 'University of the Third Age', is a self-help organisation for people no longer in full time employment, although there is no lower (or upper) age limit, and who wish to remain physically and mentally active providing educational, creative and leisure opportunities in a friendly environment. Generally it is not something that many had heard about or was relevant until they reached that time of life.

It consists of local U3As all over the UK, which are charities in their own right and are run entirely by volunteers. The website states "Local U3As are learning cooperatives which draw upon the knowledge, experience and skills of their own members to organise and provide interest groups in accordance with the wishes of the membership. The teachers learn and the learners teach". Between them U3As offer the chance to study over 300 different subjects. Currently there are 974 branches in towns and villages with over 360,000 members and continually growing.

A typical U3A has about 250 members but could be as small as 12 and as large as 2000! In Preston we have just over 500 members. The U3A approach to learning is – learning for pleasure. There is no accreditation or validation and there are no assessments or qualifications to be gained."

It is based on 'interest groups' in centres across Britain and other countries, the majority of the activities taking place during the daytime. Its main philosophy is that there is a huge wealth of knowledge and experience that can be passed on to other members in those interest groups. Whilst some groups were inaugurated 30 years ago most have only been in existence for less than ten years and in the national biannual publication – 'Third Age Matters' there are always new U3A groups starting out – each having complete independence as to what it actually does.

I can thoroughly recommend the U3A and much of the remainder of the book supplies information about the happenings of the branch in Preston. There is something for everyone and a particular benefit for members who are on their own. Whilst all kinds of clubs throughout the land have considerable difficulty in getting younger members to help, this is not an issue here as none of us fall into that category and could argue "What would we do instead?"

Regularly when they have been attending for a couple of years many recruits are happy to make a contribution by volunteering their services or initiating an interest group of their own assisted by the expertise of our Group Coordinator. A fair proportion formerly had a background in education. Most make use of the excellent facilities on offer at St Cuthbert's church, which provides a wide range of services for the local community, and other local venues. As well as the main hall, side rooms are available that can hold about twenty persons. The leader's home is used for a couple of undertakings where the number of adherents is small.

Every month there is speaker who presents a programme for an hour or so on a wide variety of subjects. These take place at the Great Room at Preston North End because of its ability to provide space for well over 100 members and visitors. There is plenty of parking and buses stop directly outside. Guests and prospective new members attending are made especially welcome by the committee and leaders. Coach excursions to places of interest are regularly organized

Music is so popular that to cope with the numbers attending, has now been split into three groups, running on different days. An assortment of themes and all styles of music are catered for. There are Singing for Pleasure and a recently formed Recorder Group that meets twice a month for those who learnt at school or always fancied being taught to play an instrument and to read music. Keyboard players are also well served with tuition for beginners and help for accomplished players.

Those with a literary or theatrical leaning are provided for by two Reading sections (also expanded because of high numbers), Poetry Appreciation and Writing, Play-reading, Drama groups, Philosophy and Discussions. Regularly members from the musical and histrionic sectors entertain us at the Christmas and other gatherings with a performance of topics that they had been rehearsing.

Local History is another aspect that had to be divided owing to an increasing attendance. As well as popular talks, outings are arranged to historical places in the North West and several meetings on matters with more general appeal that generate a wider audience use the main hall.

Those who wish to partake in more energetic activities are well provided for. Men and women do stretching and aerobic exercises with an instructor at the Keep Fit sessions. There are cycling, crown green bowling, table tennis, two rambles each month and an easy walk, at a more leisurely pace, led by volunteers. It must be stressed that these are for fun and not for the super fit who want to stretch themselves to the limit. In fact the Cycling entry on website has the warning:

Do you fancy yourself as a budding Sir Bradley Wiggins or Victoria Pendleton? Then I'm afraid we don't want to know you thank you!!! We operate a far more sedate cycling group where lycra is not de rigeur! Yes we may go up to 12 miles on our jaunts but we take our time and proceed at the rate of the slowest cyclist.

We always arrange our routes to visit a café where we partake of coffee/tea/cake/ice cream/etc. Basically, anything they have to offer! We ask that you have cycled before but emphasise we are 'recreational' cyclists not budding professionals!

Folk Dancing and the newly initiated Line Dancing are very well attended. The whole ethos revolves around 'inclusion' and ensuring that everyone is welcome.

Board games and cards are ever popular. Bridge twice a month and a session each for whist and canasta along with chess, scrabble, mah-jong and assistance with crossword solving. We have a special membership at the Stephen Hendry snooker and pool club for those who wish to hit the baize.

Other specific interest groups include Flower Arranging, Gardening, Bird Watching, Crafts, Art Appreciation, Family History and Genealogy with a mixture of indoor and outdoor visits to places of interest.

Conversational and beginners classes offer help for the linguists who like to brush up or acquire new skills in French, German, Italian and Russian and perhaps surprisingly Latin has a large following with separate sections for beginners and 'established'.

Particularly poignant is 'Moving-on'. This is a bereavement group where members, having taken the first step in joining, can meet others who are similarly learning to cope with a loss in a sympathetic manner. The leader is a trained bereavement counsellor. The Luncheon Club particularly enables those members who are on their own to dine out with pleasant company.

The Computing Group exists to introduce the world of computers to the members who would like to increase their knowledge or just so that they can find their way around the laptop or tablet and become familiar with using emails and the internet. The experts put newsletters and other items of interest onto the website and twice a year help to put together the *Good Times* publication that gives details of the programme for every activity taking place in the area. Special sessions have been run to grant access and demonstrate how those who are willing to add their own information to the web.

The latest additions are Technology and Wine Appreciation. There are dozens more topics around the country but fresh ideas require a willing teacher with the necessary know how.

Other activities take place. We run a quiz once or twice a year, organized first aid training and coffee mornings where anybody is welcome to look in and see what we have on offer. Recipe days enable members and visitors to sample the gastronomic delights of the culinary experts amongst us.

Commemorative days celebrate special occasions such as the 70th anniversary of VE Day in 1945 and themes such as Australia Day when members dress in appropriate costumes, show slides of views across the country, wildlife, art and music. An example of a previous topic was Heidi-Hi – Good Morning Switzerland, with demonstrations of how to yodel and helpings of Apple strudel, Swiss Roll and Toblerone cake. We express extreme gratitude to everyone who works tirelessly to make these events happen.

Although not something that we like to give much thought to, there frequently comes a time when an existing property becomes too large and difficult to maintain and there is a need to downsize. In recent years retirement villages have been springing up, especially formulated for the over 55s who wish to remain independent. They offer a range of amenities often with a garden, social activities, a communal lounge and access to a control centre 24 hours a day. A large percentage also provide optional meals. Obviously this is a huge decision, requiring a lot of thought and not something to be done on the spur of the moment.

We look back and ponder on just how lucky we have been throughout our lifetimes. Unlike our fathers and grandparents we have not had to fight in two world wars and unlike our seniors by less than ten years have not had to do national service.

We do not live in those parts of the world that suffer from earthquakes, droughts, severe forest fires or violent totalitarian regimes.

We could afford to put down a deposit for a house without much difficulty and have seen our standard of living soar and hopefully can now benefit from the rise in life expectancy.

Over forty years ago futuristic programmes such as *Tomorrow's World* predicted that by now we would be living in a world with robots in every home and even vehicles taking to the air as in the Jetsons and that we would only be needing to work for a few hours, a couple of days a week. Needless to say this hasn't happened. The nation works longer hours, wastes more time travelling and the digital world, the internet and everyday appliances such as mobile phones were never foreseen.

However the pace of change has never been faster. Driverless cars may be only a few years away, drones and robotics a step nearer, anticipated to revolutionise jobs in every area of life not merely in connection with machines in factories.

Advances in medicine predict 3D printers able to manufacture body parts. Nanotechnology will allow the manipulation of genes to treat cancers without surgery or chemotherapy, new research to prevent dementia and devices that can be worn to monitor our health. The paralysed able to walk with prosthetic limbs responding to human thought.

Electronic newspapers are envisaged soon along with solar powered planes and developments that we cannot conceive of today. It is unlikely that many of us oldies will be around to see if these prophesies materialise.

There are countless problems facing our descendants. Global warming and combatting terrorism immediately spring to mind.

We all wish that we had had the opportunity to do things that for all sorts of reasons were not possible or taken a different decision that would have had a major impact on our lives. Our blazer at primary school had an emblem stating 'Carpe diem' or seize the day and grasp your opportunity. Hopefully we have made the best of things with few regrets and can still put our many years of experience to benefit others.

Having a variety of activities to fill our days, meet new friends and try to do what we can is the best way to be happy and ensure that we have never had it so good!